THE ANCHORAGE

BERNARD O'DONOGHUE

The Anchorage

faber

First published in 2025
by Faber & Faber Ltd
The Bindery, 51 Hatton Garden
London EC1N 8HN

Typeset by Hamish Ironside
Printed in the UK by Martins the Printers

A CIP record for this book is available from the British Library

ISBN 978-0-571-38793-9

MIX
Paper | Supporting
responsible forestry
FSC
www.fsc.org
FSC™ C013254

Printed and bound in the UK on FSC® certified paper in line with our continuing
commitment to ethical business practices, sustainability and the environment.
For further information see faber.co.uk/environmental-policy

Our authorised representative in the EU for product safety is
Easy Access System Europe, Mustamäe tee 50, 10621 Tallinn, Estonia
gpsr.requests@easproject.com

2 4 6 8 10 9 7 5 3 1

in memory of Margaret MacCarron

Calling out, as is the custom of those who go often in the woods,
'Where are you now, companion?'

— AELFRIC, *The Life of St Edmund*

Acknowledgements

Acknowledgements are due to the editors of the following, in which versions of several of these poems first appeared: *14 Magazine*, edited by Richard Skinner; *Agenda*; *Fragile*, edited by Ian Heames; *Irish Examiner*; *Irish Times*; *New Statesman*; *Oxford Magazine*; *Poetry Ireland Review*; *Poetry London*; *The Quince* (Oriel College, Oxford); *Times Literary Supplement*; *Western People*; *Wild Court*, edited by Robert Selby; *Winchester Festival Magazine*; *Yale Review*. 'Topdress' was published in *The Elements in the Medieval World: Interdisciplinary Perspectives: Earth*, edited by M. Cesario, H. Magennis and E. Ramazzina (Brill); 'Safe Houses' was published in *Lives of Houses*, edited by Kate Kennedy and Hermione Lee (Princeton University Press); 'At the Wimpy Bar on Cornmarket' was published in *Postcards from the Archive*, edited by Heidi Williamson (Rothermere American Institute, Oxford); 'Homesickness' was published in *Reading Gender and Space: Essays for Patricia Coughlan*, edited by Anne Fogarty and Tina O'Toole (Cork University Press); 'Lepus' was published in *Reading the Future: New Writing from Ireland Celebrating 250 Years of Hodges Figgis*, edited by Alan Hayes (Arlen House); 'The Privee Theef' was published in *Poems on Conflict* (Chough Publications); 'Beara Skylines' and 'Pruning in August' were published in *Five Poems by Bernard O'Donoghue* (Clutag Press).

Contents

THE ANCHORAGE

Rough Plaster

We spend our summers in a house once owned
By a couple who never spoke a word
To each other. And we have wondered if,
Mixed in with the rough plaster on the walls,
Some bitter trace still lingers. But in their day
There was no window on to the southern hills,
No song from the music system, and no one
Calling from upstairs for a weather forecast
That will tell us if it's fine enough for the sea.

Pre-check-in

It's always the same dream before you travel:
Cases not packed, unsorted contents
Thrown on the bed. The others don't seem to have
Remembered the time, or to care:
Down in the restaurant, with everything
Still to do. The taxi has been booked,
But will it be on time? Or will it wait?
And what time does the check-in have to close?

Like the man from Coalpits who set off too soon
To walk to the train for the journey to Queenstown
And America because of the early crowing
Of the neighbour's cock through some strange disorder.
'Bad luck to you, Dan Cronin, and your fowl!
I could have spent those last few hours at home.'

The Anchorage

One morning in the hot summer of '59
We watched through binoculars a black cloud
Of smoke on the skyline. Someone suggested
It must be furze being burned on the banks
Of the railway line. Word spread
That it was Bill Casey's barn, new-packed
With this year's hay. We all went to see it,
And smelled the dead smell of burning.
Casey kicked ruefully at the iron staple
In the wall which the dog had been chained to.
All the farmers in the parish rallied round;
The next Sunday a long cortège of horse floats
Made their slow way along the dusty road
To Ardnageeha to repair the loss.
But what good was that? The barn's dark pillars
Did not lighten, and when you closed your eyes
What you saw was the invisible
Last leaping of the dog.

The Hide

from Old Irish

Than our small observatory in Túaim Inbir
no great mansion could be better
with stars in due order
and sun and moon.

It was the Gobán that made it
so his fame would be passed down.
My dear heart, God in Heaven,
He is the thatcher who made the roof.

A house into which the rain can't pour,
a refuge where no spear-point's feared,
open and bright to a garden
with no wattle fence around it.

While the Sun Shines

for Hugh Haughton

In the meadows of the dead they're hard at work,
Anxious to get the hay up before the weather breaks.
Everyone's involved: people of all ages
With two-pronged pikes, the older prongs
Shortened by years of use. They work with
Every horse-drawn mechanism:
Wheel rake, swath-turner and tumbling paddy,
The skeeter with its treacherous steel teeth
Which cut bloody parallel lines down shins.
At the edge of the group are tall men
Wielding long-handled rakes with wooden teeth,
Some missing, some replaced by twigs of elder,
Combing up the wisps missed by the gatherers.

I don't recognise them all, but some I do.
Some I recall the names of, but can't remember
Which of them the name attaches to. None
Can I distract from their activity.
'We can't stop now,' they say. 'There's too much still to do.'

Folk Tale

for Lucy and Frank

I wish I'd never started on this story;
It may have been a dream, or maybe not:
We're driving home from Cork one winter's evening
And join a queue of traffic at the Sandpit,
At the corner where the chimney used to stand
That we thought was a Round Tower. A Guard,
Swinging a lamp, came up to the car window,
Motioning to wind it down. He told us
A lorry had shed its load of beet. We could wait
For half an hour or more, or work backwards
All the way round Kanturk. And that was what
We did: down by the Protestant chapel at Dromagh –
Sold, they say, for nine hundred pounds,
The value of the leadwork on the roof,
On by the high back road to Boherbue,
Past Derrygallon where Kate Mac had gone
To school. The stories she used to tell us! –
The teacher's spoilt daughter, with ribbons
In her hair, who was always brought to school
In a horse and trap; the two young neighbours
On the run, hiding in the turf-shed at the back;
The time that Jer was driving home in the trap
(They must then have still been on speaking terms)
One dark night and felt breathing behind him,
A presence, as of someone by the backboard.
As we dropped down towards the Araglen,
At the point where years ago we used to see
The dim glow of the poacher's lantern,
Night was falling fully, and we were glad

To turn at last into our own front yard,
Welcomed by the Christmas tree
With its artificial lights framed in the window.

Firelighters

His house was so wet and cold in winter
there was no question of doing without a fire.
But how did people start a fire again?
Place the packet of Zip cubes in the grate
and strike a match. Briefly the room lit up,
and a friendly warmth embraced him, enough
nearly to make him sing. But it didn't last:
a few minutes, and it was dark again.
This was how it had always been: the flare
of friendship or acclaim – 'Sound, O'Connor!' –
in the pub, followed by the normal
indifference and neglect. So he'd pull
the soaking blanket over him and wait
for the cold, unfeeling light at break of day.

Lif is laene

You must read the small print and the rubric
for the strict terms on which they're given to us.
We only have them on approval,
so for God's sake I say to love them
and not for themselves. They are on loan;
we must be prepared to send them back
if we're not ready for the high investment
of their keeping. And you must not put
their pictures into albums till you're sure
you can bear the cost of items
of such inestimable value.

Pruning in August

In China, a cherished gardening skill
is to prune the shrubs in such a way that
it's imperceptible that they've been pruned
at all. But here, before departing
at summer's end, I trim off all the shoots
that might have flowered later in the year
for those who come here after us,
cutting tight to the growth rings near the base.
For, just as it always gives a pang
to throw out roses, even when their stalks
have started to soften and the blooms to bow
downward in defeat, we can't bear to think
of their display before the next comers
as if they'd never been the heart of things for us.

Trusty

for John Fitzgerald

Of the boys, only I reached sixth class
as my contemporaries were kept at home
to farm or were sent out in service.
During the summer, I was delegated
to meet the mobile library van at school
and knelt upstairs choosing the books
for the coming year: Billy Bunter,
William, The Famous Five, even Biggles;
nearer to home Patricia Lynch: *Brogeen*,
The Turf-Cutter's Donkey, *King of the Tinkers*,
The Mad O'Haras and *The Bookshop on the Quay*.

I knew what I liked myself, but had to learn
what teachers favoured – things that bore on
history or geography or folklore:
In Sarsfield's Days, *Fontenoy*, *On the Run*.
I learned to arrange the books by title
alphabetically, by subject and by size,
before lining them up in due order
next to the ink-powder cartons in the spare classroom.

Next Time

Every morning he came in by the back door
which was always on the latch. Without a word
he'd pick up *The Examiner*, hold it
at arm's length, glasses perched on the end
of his long nose. He read the paper
from the back, starting attentively
with the deaths, then the sports pages
which did not detain him long, only pausing
when it described the feats of Tadhgie Lyne,
the son of his cattle-dealing colleague.
On each occasion he was asked 'You'll have
a cup of tea?' and he'd answer 'Next time',
pick up his stick and stalk out the front,
best foot forward, into the yard.

God the Landlord

for Rosie and Martin

Although he never appeared behind the bar,
we believed in his existence because things
happened which otherwise were inexplicable:
beer-barrels were changed, bags of crisps replaced,
and the licence was still issued in his name.
But we did see him once, on the feast
of the Epiphany, by the bus stop
in Millstreet, wearing a jaunty hat,
all joviality, as he set off
on the first leg of his trip to London
where he had lived for twenty years,
humming now *Emmanuel, Emmanuel.*

Stanley Gibbons

On the inside cover of my uncle's album
it says 'For dear Hugh with fondest love from
Father and Mother, 1923.'
Throughout the discoloured pages
are spattered low denomination
commonplaces. Occasionally
next to a smudge where gummed hinges had been
there appears a pencilled note
'Gibbons 4/6'; or 'may be valuable'.
I can see him now at a later point: striding out
hopefully in his unbelted mack
to show them to an informed philatelist
with a magnifying glass who shakes his head
and hands them back, leaving him
to find another way to raise the money
for another afternoon drinking alone.

Rule-Breakers

That summer, when the Rings above in Doon
took the chance of the one fine day, a Sunday,
to make up the hay, we watched across the valley
from our hens' field where we played football,
hearing the periodic rattle
of the big hay-rake's metal wheels,
amplified in the breeze over the glen
as they piked and trimmed in the middle distance
in troubling violation of the Sabbath.

Football wasn't work. The only time
I remember my father imposing
any prohibition was a Sunday when he came
from the house and said 'Stop playing now.
Din Keeffe is dead.' Another time
he led me into the Protestant church
in Ballybunion, though we'd been told
at school it was a sin to go to such a place.

And one Lenten Sunday, having held out
for thirty days, I recklessly bought
in Jack the Clerk's shop a Club biscuit,
thickly covered in forsworn milk chocolate.
It tasted not of ash, but of something worse:
the sweet poison of a chosen vow broken.

L'Aiuola

L'aiuola che ci fa tanto feroci
– DANTE, *Paradiso* 22, 151

In the morning it was raining, so
we were sent unwillingly to school.
But when it dried up before midday
the thresher made its lumbering way along
the road past the playground, its pale pink
a slow glimpse through the blackthorn hedges.
Was it coming for us? Then a miracle:
our father's hat framed in the dim glass
of the classroom half-door, motioning to us.
Had he left the busy threshing floor behind
to drive the mile to school to bring us back
for this most essential feast day of the year?

When, later, Theresa died in hospital
my mother had to go to break the news.
'Theresa is not good, Jula.' 'Must we go to Cork?'
'She's worse than that, Jula.' So they drove to school
to bring her sister and her brothers home.
It was not a busy scene of threshing
they brought them to, but the flower garden
that Theresa had tended all her short life.

The Privee Theef

We'd always heard he walked the land round here:
Mostly some miles away, but now he's
Rumoured to be closer. In one village
He was said to have attacked woman, child,
Householder and servant. So why don't they
Do something about it? Raid his furtive camp
And kick asunder his pots and pans
Amid the greying ashes,
The utensils in which he brews his potions;
Or strike out boldly with knife and gun.
I hesitate to put a name to him
Because that way he's won. Better to let on
You don't know.
Meanwhile in our neighbouring country
They are taking the locks off the doors
So the refugees can find some refuge there.

Remote Control

I wasn't there; but I can see it still –
how the trusting dog was held down
as the vet carefully injected
a fatal bubble into his bloodstream
so he died at once. And this was because
I, three hundred miles away, could not live
with not knowing what he was doing,
every hour of every day, where he'd bounded,
tongue lolling, towards me across the field.

The Lickowen Myrtle

for Andreas Flückiger, Schlossstrasse 144

Despite repeated efforts to transplant it
we've failed to make it ever take root here
so far inland. By now we struggle
to recall its species or its seaboard origin.
The time is coming when we won't remember
even the spelling of its donor's name –
yours, who made it grow in such profusion
with the unwavering devotion
of a newcomer to the island's climate.
We'll need no more to feel anxiety
about your safety on the narrow path
to the end of Toe Head promontory
where you led us, natives all, in single file,
as the Blasket Islanders walked the streets
of Dingle in a cautious line, as if
they'd never left the rocky slope above
the perilous sheer drop down to the sea.

Rakings and Cleanings

for Nicky Grene

I

When the whole field of haycocks was made up,
sometimes as many as forty in three acres,
we'd make a last wynd from the wisps left over
from the raking down of the completed ones
that stood like Wagner's giants in the twilight.

We always had to note which wynd that was:
it never held its place among the rest,
but retained an incompleteness to it,
like a page of scraps of half-abandoned thoughts,
or a story that you wish you'd never started.

And when it was brought in, last, to the barn,
it was never piked on to the big ricks
but pushed to the edge near the corrugated rim
to guard the better hay from contact
with the winter's rain that causes grass to rot.

2

After the big haycock had been hauled onto the float,
you'd pick up the damp clump from the base
where it had made contaminating contact
with the ground, and you'd tuck it at the back,

held by the rope that was flung diagonally
over the top to the front corner. This too would fail
to reach the sweet-smelling ricks in the haybarn,
but would join a lesser pile at the yard's corner

for use as bedding for the calves in winter,
while the hay-knife blade sang through
the blocks cool and dry
leaving an edge as keen as a new haircut.

The Pulsator

It was rare for people other than family
To stay overnight with us: two Poor Clares from Manchester
On one occasion; once a White Father
With a bulbous motor scooter
Who'd met our cousin out on the Missions;
Two lady teachers from Shakespeare's Stratford
Who didn't stay in the house, puzzlingly
Sleeping in their camper van on the grass outside.

But when the Simplex milking machine went wrong
A man called Joyce from Galway came to check
The Pulsator, which always seemed
To be the trouble. On the Sunday morning
My mother knocked on his bedroom door
And asked if he wanted to get up for Mass,
But he said that he was 'Church of Ireland',
And turned his back.

Largesse

Cullen 1 was the exchange at the Post Office
Where Loretta filtered and enabled
Incoming and outgoing calls. Cullen 2
Was the Creamery where they took orders
For ration and issued the milk-account books
Of folded canvas. We had the next phone
Because our father drove from here to Dingle
And up to Kerry Head, selling insurance.
We were where the neighbours had to come
To ring for inseminators or the vet.

Sometimes the number led to a confusion
With the Cistercian Monastery in County Louth,
Also Cullen 3. We used to picture
A Brother picking up the phone to listen
To a Cork accent wondering if the order
For ringworm treatment was yet in stock.

A generation later, here in Oxford,
Bent-backed Tony with his neat straw hat
And clipped vowels came daily to our house
To ring for a taxi to take him home
From the house of blind Miss Monk where she wept
Amid her countless starving cats,
Back to his flat in Princes Street.
Mostly we waved away the shilling payment:
'How kind you always are!' he'd say to us.

Substitute Driver

for Győző Ferencz

Before the days of seatbelts, I could sit
Holding to the dashboard to see out,
Despite the warnings not to bang my head.
And when my father went into the shop
Or the Creamery Store, I could start the
Wipers to clear the drops of rain
That settled on the windscreen, until,
Because the engine was switched off, they slowed
And slowed and stopped at a slant.
'Don't do it,' he said. 'You'll flatten the battery.'
But I wasn't ready to give up my guard
Over those rubber blades as they juddered
Slower and slower until at last they
Came to a conclusive standstill in mid-stroke.

Back on the Island

i.m. Mícheál Ó Súilleabháin

Behind the mysterious ground of the cellos,
tunes were secreted, waiting to break out
and dance on the keys: 'The Three Sea-Captains',
'Cooley's' or 'Killarney Boys of Pleasure'.
How did he know where they were?
He must have put them there himself:
it's the only explanation. When things are lost,
we keep on looking in places where we know
they are not because we've looked there already.
But they remain the most likely places:
back on the island, we'll look there again.

Time to Go

for Tereza and Jiri

The directions from the people at reception
were clear enough, uninterested though they seemed,
and the porter led me straight up to my room.
Throughout my stay, when I came back in
from sightseeing, I returned there
with relief: third floor, five doors to the left.
But on the day set for my departure
I must have got out at the wrong floor because
when I got to the room, the door was open
and a case – not mine – lay open on the bed.
The cleaner was busy in the bathroom, humming,
and a bored-looking young woman sat
in the armchair, leafing through a magazine.
'Isn't this my room?' I asked. She shrugged and said
'I don't know. I guess when you've settled up
down at the desk, then you'll be free to go.'

The Funeral

Not a mark on its sheer glossy blackness,
its wings still swept back, its frame bone-light.
Heart failure maybe, or a silent blow.
In the evening they began to come in numbers
from all directions, as if summoned
by a bell to pay observance, crying
in harsh protestation and lament.
They circled and swooped
before perching at the gable, reaching forward to call
as if their lives depended on it.
By the time night fell they'd all departed,
north towards Taur or southeast to Mushera
where I picture them settled again,
ready for sleep among the pines.

Cargo Cults

We crossed the step to take the milk to Nora
every evening before the dark set in
and crossed back with the owl's call in our ears.
Why was Donal's dog barking? Was he hearing
the fox on its early exploration
of the ditch by the hens' field? From further off
came the call of the heron we'd never seen
outside the pages of an English children's book
sent by our grandmother from Manchester.
Some birds, we learned, had never made it across
the Irish Sea: the woodpecker,
jay or nuthatch. But we could barter with our own:
the *bonnán buí* whose cold laying-out
promoted the grace of a happy death
but sorrow too; the snipe that dived
down the sky below his drumming;
and the drowned blackbird for whose tragedy
the daughter of the O'Neills cried day and night.

Safe Houses

I find that I have started recently
to keep spare keys to the front door
in several pockets, such is my fear
of being locked out. Caught by the wind
the door could shut quietly behind you,
leaving you to face the outer world alone.
But once safe inside I don't put on the chain.

In civil wars, the combatants
change their safe house at intervals
to give their hosts a rest from listening
for the thump on the door in the early hours,
as at the end of winter you escape
from cold and dark by making for
the sunnier climates to the south.

But where do we retreat to in the end
when the call to open up will not subside?
Kate in her nineties was no longer fit
to mind herself, so they took her in
to the Lee Road. When I called to see her
the nurse unlocked the door to the main room
and turned the key again behind me.

And there she was, with twenty others,
all chattering and laughing like a parliament
of magpies, not to each other
but to the unhearing world outside.
I thought of Masaccio's grieving couple,
not grasping what they've been exiled from,
some corner where the serpent cannot reach.

Kate's Magic Egg

All her Sunday-evening women visitors
were taken down to The Room to see it:
her little Taj Mahal of green plastic.
Its parallel grooves required her good nails
and careful fingering to open the top,
remove the white round egg and place it
in full view on the table, shake the container
vigorously, pronouncing the words of the spell,
and lo and behold! when she opened it again
another white egg, plain to be seen!

Her niece Nora Quinn, her closest relative,
had bought it at Woolworths in Reading
in those days when you could not find
such magic for love nor money in our neck
of the woods. But after Kate was moved
to her magnolia prefab in the village,
and from there on to the County Home,
where has it gone to work its magic since?

Thanks, though

i.m. Margaret

The dream always the same: I'm listening to
The latest CD you sent – Matt Cranitch,
Or Ó Riada, or Mná an Oileáin.
I want to ring to thank you; but I can't
Find your number anywhere. And then
I remember: you changed your mobile
The week before you died, so now of course
I can't get through. And – something I hadn't
Noticed before – this CD is defective.
I take it out and rinse it under the tap,
But it makes no difference.
It still judders at the same point, just before
Séamus Begley starts on 'Aisling Gheal'.

Walking the Land

In the days before the auction of the farm
that cold March of 1962,
I led potential buyers through the fields,
showing them the bounds and listening
to their evaluation of the soil.
The good land was to the front of the house:
the Gate Field; Jackson's; the Western Field;
the Stone Field where the standing stone
had been bulldozed into the quarry.
The Cottage Field stretched to the east,
by the lazy-bed ridges of the Well Field
where the dog bounded to greet you,
his hope-filled eyes dazzling.
To the north was the Screen Field and the Furzy Glen
where we had seen long-eared owls
winging mystically through the twilight.
Below the pink spreading hawthorn in Murt's Field
was the Guttery Gap into the Quarry Field
that led to Dominic's Inch where we used to gather
frail mushrooms in the dawn along the river.
But none of these were considerations
that weighed much with the shrewd and thoughtful men
who were pondering a bid for our farmland.

At the Wimpy Bar on Cornmarket

He has nodded off, his big head drooping
towards his knees, the half-drunk half-bottle
of whiskey sloping from the pocket
of his withered sports coat. From the next table
a young man reached over with a wink,
furtively extricated the bottle
from the pocket and passed it along
to his friend. You stopped what you were saying,
sprang to your feet and shouted:
'Put it back. It's his. Give it back to him.'
At once they did, the whole thing unknownst to him:
this intervention on behalf of rights
he'd never understood he had or not.

Lepus

I thought I heard a car in the early hours,
stealing down the road beneath the window
with its engine cut. But when I came downstairs
to see if it was parked in the front yard,
there was nothing there. Puzzled, I headed back
towards bed; but when I reached the landing
with its westlin view across the fields
over Glounthaune, I saw a blue mountain hare
on the stones behind the house, a visitant
that the earlier dwellers here
would see as a messenger or harbinger
of doom. It sensed my presence, and turned
back to the road by which no car had come
past fuchsia, willowherb and clematis.
I got back into bed and dreamed of airports
and ferries and a failed attempt to keep
the tail-lights of the car ahead in view.

Madonna

The downturned face of the young woman
Across from us on the bus, illuminated
By the light from her mobile phone, is like
That of a seventeenth-century virgin at the heart
Of the picture. Such will you have been
At some in-between time, now long after
That cold St Brigid's Day when I found you
At the Queen's Lane bus stop, your fingers
With the same bare bloom as hers.
But you were crying, impatient
To be alone, your copper hair pulled back
By the wind as you urgently waved me off
With that still-loved, still-unrecaptured hand.

Topdress

Those daffodils that grew in frail clusters
in our back haggard in North Cork – who planted them,
and how had they survived without nutrition
either from us or from the crumbling orange shale
above the quarry? They made their way through,
as poppies grow unaccountably in clay
from East Anglia to Flanders.
Some things we did transplant: primroses
whose roots we pulled out in heavy hanks
from the roadside by the well,
and wiry mauve heather from the mountain.
But they all lost heart after our time
and left when we did, the coast clear
for the unaccountable narcissi.

2

Yet surely it was progress when we left
the toil and trade of farming in the rushes
to set off in the sun to Fog Lane Park
kept impeccably by Manchester Council,
past the manicured edges of the flower-beds
where the heavy mowers hummed all day
with the bees among the rhododendrons.
On past the matt-green kiosk where you paid
to play on the raked pink shale tennis courts
near the immaculate lawn for crown green bowling.
Topdress was the term we used for the
rank foul-smelling dung we spread as
nutrient on vegetable beds back at home.
That can't be what achieved perfection here.

3

Christ Church Meadow didn't go by the rule:
long-horned cattle in its rushy central field
and black reflecting water by the path,
as if it were Jer Mac's long coarse meadow
with dank rush drains down along its edges.
How had the wildness and the wet survived
in such a place of ageless cultivation?
We even found there the grace of Lady's Smock
and breathed again the scent of primroses
that we had tried to bring to mind by
closing our eyes. When we went back home, in turn
we mowed the grass and trimmed the berberis
around the foundations that marked the place
where the cattle stall and the stolid barn had stood.

4

In Manchester briefly for a funeral,
before we made our way out to the airport
there was just time to visit Fog Lane Park.
The grass was growing knee-high to the gate
and we could hardly see where the borders were.
No gardeners knelt by the flower beds, where
patches of country grass had turned to withered grey,
grown long and thin around the elder trees,
untended, uncut, unharvested. *Tara is grass*
and behold how Troy lies low. But listen
to the wind, and half-believe it carries the echo
of the hay float's ratchet and the call *How! How!*
to the cows coming in for milking.

Jim Cronin Recalls his Parting from Denis Hickey

He never ventured farther than the door
to see me out. But that June night of song thrush
and flowering currant he said 'I'll convey you
to the gate'. He didn't stop by the dog
to urge him to jump on the milk stand
so he could say 'Broch, give me the paw',
but he walked on without a word to the end
of the path. And he didn't raise
his arm or click his heels in mock salute
when I started the engine. I thought again
of all these minor differences
three days later at the memorial Mass,
and when we lowered his coffin into the earth.

Homesickness

Her heart was bad – or so they always said –
and she couldn't face the chapel the cold day
of her favourite daughter's funeral. But how
could they be sure that the view from the window
of the cortège passing would not kill her?
Her next-door neighbour – a midwife famous for
her tact and skill at sympathy –
would seat her with her back turned to the road
and prompt discussion of her favourite topic:
Manhattan before nineteen twenty-nine.
Tears came to her eyes as she recalled
the skyscrapers above the narrow streets.
'You'd go into Central Park on the West Side,
and it could take you half an hour and more
before you'd come out by the museums to the East.
And you should see the view from the very top
of the Empire State Building. I remember still the day
of the Wall Street Crash as if it was yesterday.
Nothing else in the papers for a week.
It took everybody's mind off everything.'
The minder kept a wary eye on the hearse
creeping past and on all the bowed heads
of friends and cousins walking with sad steps.
The bells tolled through the midday sleet.
The minder pictured the mourners by the grave:
the coffin lowered; the tears of the relations.
But still Mamie nodded at the fire,
well beyond the reach of grief.

Countryside Alliance

Train up your youth to hunt and shoot
With a dog and gun to go
To kill the game that still remain
Where the Mulcair river flows.
— attrib. JAMES RYAN OF DOON

You could never pass the church-door table
Where they collected for worthy causes:
St Vincent de Paul for poor relief,
The Diocesan Seminary,
The Irish Countrywomen's Association
Of which my Manchester mother was the Chair.
Although she swore that every year would be
Her last, she was always reappointed.

The men of the parish you admired the most –
The county footballers and the musicians,
Men who gave you Confirmation money –
Manned the table for the Coursing Club.
Would they understand it when you slipped
Past them with a smile and put nothing
On the plate? But how could you explain
You'd not become an enemy, or lost your faith
In them? That it didn't mean that you would not
Turn out still to cheer them on with pride
At the next big match? How could you care less
For them than for a wild hare that dodged
This way and that to escape their cherished dogs?

Immortelles

When they broke the door down
They found the carnations still there
On the kitchen table where at the end of summer
They must have seemed too vibrant
To throw out. So there they'd stayed,
Unlooked at and unwatered through the autumn.
It wasn't easy to remember
What they were, those dry, rebuking twigs
And shrivelled blossoms, standing next to
A candelabra of wilted tulips.

Meccano Magazine

Bridge May Riordan ordered it for me
From London. Being educational,
It was exempt from the 2d import tax,
Which was ironic because in the reading
Of instructions, I was ineducable.
The sons of the creamery manager,
Who also had Set 5, completed models
So they always came out exactly like
The detailed illustration in the brochure:
The Bridge over the River Kwai; an Alpine
Funicular railway; a working crane;
And they never had an unused piece left over,
Having put every item to its minute purpose.
I still find in drawers and boxes, under
The carpet or behind the skirting board,
The occasional small screw, nut or clip
That should have contributed to some grander whole.

Calendar Customs

If I could be bothered, I would write it down,
taking note of what I'd planted where,
or where after May the briars would close in
and choke the shrubs. But I've always chosen
not to: to let them all take their chance
and maybe create the circumstances
when someone, fifty years from now, will come
upon a berberis, rose or lily
in some unlikely place, just as I found,
fifty years ago, a strawberry plant
where you'd least expect it, in the ragged
back half-acre behind the old screen.

Unbroken Dreams

Qual è colui che somniando vede,
che dopo il sogno la passione impressa
rimane, e l'altro alla mente non riede;

cotal son io, chè quasi tutta cessa
mia visione, ed ancor mi distilla
nel cor lo dolce che nacque da essa.

          – DANTE, *Paradiso* 33, 58–63

It seemed we had done with all that: attained
peace of mind, accepting that the body
cannot outlive its one material death
and that its shapeless fellow traveller, the mind,
goes with it. There is no longer any need
to fear eternal suffering.

But could death not strike while you are mid-dream
so you remain at that point for ever:
at the culmination, for example,
of the nightmare in which, having jumped
from ship rail or tower block, you go on
falling like Mulciber *from Morn*
to Noon but never hit the water or the ground?
Or it might be while you're dreaming of
a late reconciliation where she says
you could meet after all, so you remain
suspended in hope for all eternity.
It's more secure the way things seem to be,
where you can sit a while on the concrete path
behind the house before the sun declines
below the west, into its civil twilight.

The Skellig Listeners

for Paddy Bushe

The boatman said, fine as it was that morning,
there'd be no boats the next day, eight miles out
in the weather, with a force seven whipping up seas
wild enough to discourage Vikings.
But this day had broken blue and bright,
and when we disembarked we had to shelter
from the sun. The birds were all out to sea.

The medieval bards were locked away
in light-proof rooms until the poem was done.
Wanting to learn inspiration from the birds –
these storm-dwelling cousins of the albatross
that spend their winters in the Southern Ocean –
we too lay low until the night
could raise the cover to grow dark.

Even at eleven o'clock when we looked out
that night of June, it was still not dark enough
for shearwaters to make their noiseless return
from the outer deep. So we waited
until midnight before climbing up
the six hundred steps to the monastery
to start our vigil. We didn't catch them

in the act: but, as watchers for sunrise
are suddenly aware that it has dawned
though they haven't seen the sun rising,
we knew that they were there: that somehow,
no pace perceived, they'd filled the whole night
with wings above our heads, and all around
we listened to the anxious revenants.

More wonderful, every crevice by the beehive huts
was filled with the sound of petrels. As we picked our way
down the steps, sheer over the Atlantic,
we had to be careful not to trample them,
sprawling ungainly in the corners
as they shrank away from us on their hopeless legs,
claiming refuge on the rock that was their home.

Maker

i.m. Pat Joe Morley

Of all the virtues, he had least time for patience.
When the tension of the closing stages
in the match became unbearable,
he'd seize his cap and set off down the fields
with the dogs. Or when the days indoors
dragged on, he'd take off out to the shed
to fiddle with the tuning of the tractor
or to sand down the rungs of a wooden chair.
He learned to know the durability
of wood from its grain. His first job
had been making coffins in Kildare;
in his good times, he said, he could make
a dozen in a day, sawing and planing
and varnishing until night fell.
He told me he had broken every finger
at least once in a lifetime of building
hay-barns and staircases and kitchen cabinets
all through the county, as he worked
to leave the world better than he found it.

Sandpipers at Rosslare

for Claire and Paul

The standard procedure is to fill up
with petrol just past the long scenic Sweep
down into Dungarvan, to drop the bags
at the Rosslare Lodge and drive to the beach
behind the Ferryport where our boat is
all business, preparing to set off.
It will reach Wales and then cross back for us
to embark in the morning. As the twilight
deepens, the on-off of the Tuskar Light
finds its range; we are watching a stonechat
swaying precariously on its perch.
At the water's edge a small flock of sandpipers
is pattering to and fro, letting us almost
catch up, then shrilling off in a sparkling V
of flight to settle on a new ridge of sand,
fifty yards ahead. Having escaped us
they run to the sea which in turn runs at them
so they double back. This is where they live;
it's where they will be when we next start out
from this same perfect point of departure.

Beara Skylines

Don't worry if you can't guide a steady line.
Use as your medium a 'shaky' line.
                        – BYAM SHAW to Evie Hone

I remember best the contours of the hills –
their rough-edged, rounded tops of heather purple,
the rocks behind the village worn away
like over-working molars: a perfect backdrop
looking as if there's nothing to the back of them.
The painter who coloured in this landscape
has scribbled the sea-line so that it forms
not too precise an edge against the land
where crooked fields freewheel down to the sea.

If you choose the right vantage point,
around the corner northwards on this coast,
then move up the road in second gear,
the lesser Skellig will move across the greater
so it disappears as by a sleight of hand:
then slowly reappears, a pale spirit,
inviting a polite round of applause.

Winding Up

for Mick Henry

We might choose to bring him to mind
on his high musician's stool, head held back
as he sang 'Anach Cuan' or O'Casey's 'Nora'
when violets were scenting the woods;
but I would recall him at the finish of
the evening's music, winding up
the tangled leads of his amplifiers
while the rest of us took to the streets
out of the night that he had created,
before the lights were off and he too
was free to pack up and make for home.